Stop Beating Your Meat Smoke It Instead

A BBQ Cookbook

PITMASTER GRADY TALBOT

Foreword

I cover a little bit of everything in this book because more than anything I wanted to share my top 50 recipes that I've perfected over the years. These recipes involve different smoking and grilling equipment like a smoker, traditional grill, dutchoven, and even a Sous Vide (I promise I'm not fancy, but this is one hell of a way to cook a steak!). I don't expect everyone to be grilling or smoking on an Egg. If you are, props to you, but just remember it doesn't take the best equipment to make some damn good meats. 90% of the recipes in this book have a hearty protein in it, but I do share a few side dishes that I didn't think were fair to leave out. Give them a shot and I think you'll see why. I also included a couple of desserts that will blow your freakin' minds!

When it comes to smoking meats, it can be an intimidating hobby to start. Many people who cook barbecue believe theirs is the best, and sometimes that confidence can scare people away. I am here to tell you that anyone can make great barbecue. All it takes is the right equipment, a lot of patience, and even more practice. Below is a list of tools to get you started on your journey to mouth-watering brisket, ribs, chicken, and MORE!

Table of Contents.

You will need:

A Smoker.

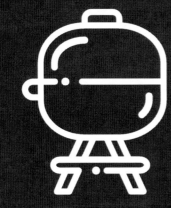

Offset smokers, Pellet smokers, and Weber-style smokers are the most common.

Charcoal.

Gas Grill.

A 3-4 burner grill is great because you'll cook some foods on indirect heat.

Dutch Oven.

Medium-sized is all you need.

Kitchen Tools.

Preferably a large cutting board.

Sharp knives

Tongs

Sauce Brush

Meat Thermometer.

Optional:

Surface Thermometer.

For locating your smokers "hot spots".

Aluminum Foil.

Some cuts of meat can be wrapped in aluminum foil to speed up the cooking process and seal in juices. This is known as the "Texas Crutch," but if you keep a steady temperature it isn't necessary.

Meat.

Brisket, Ribs, Pork Butts, Chicken, and many more types of meat can be used for barbecue.

Rubs and Sauce.

These go hand in hand, although some "purists" believe barbecue sauce to be unnecessary.

A Timer.

What to know about barbecuing:

- **Temperature Control.**

  The number one key to making great barbecue is temperature control. You can spend all the money in the world buying the best equipment, but if your smoker has drastic swings in temperature, your meat will not impress anyone. Temperature swings will lead to dry cuts of tough meat.

- **Fat Reduction.**

  What makes barbecue so tasty is melted, or "rendered" fat. Most barbecue meats are cheap and full of fat. Meaning if you were to grill it quickly, without slow and consistent heat, the fat would be chunky and unsavory. That is why temperature control is so important. Equally as important is being sure that you give the meat enough time to properly render most of the fat.

- **Patience.**

  Barbecue is very fun, however, it is important to remember that some meats can take up to 15 hours on the grill to be completely done! Brisket is the best example of this. So if you plan on making chopped beef sandwiches for the family on Sunday for lunch, you should probably begin cooking on Saturday.

Smoked.

Sandwiches, Pork, Chicken, Steak, Ribs

Forkin' Good Pulled Pork

This is by far the easiest cut of meat to smoke. Due to the high-fat content on the pork butt, also referred to as the "Boston Butt", the temperature swings will not affect the taste and texture as much. Which is why I am putting it first in the book. Let's get started!

Ingredients:

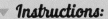

- ½ Cup Dark Brown Sugar
- ½ Cup Sweet Paprika
- ¼ Cup Thick Kosher Salt
- ⅔ Cup Chili Powder
- ¼ Cup Dry Mustard
- ½ Cup Yellow Mustard
- 1 Tbsp. Freshly Ground Black Pepper
- 2 Tbsp. Crab Boil Seasoning (Recommended: Old Bay)
- ½ Tsp. of Allspice
- 1 Cup 100% Apple Juice
- 1 Bag of Pre-packaged Coleslaw with Sesame Ginger Dressing

Instructions:

I love this recipe because of how easy it is! Get the pork butt out and rub it down with yellow mustard. Just enough to coat the outside (you don't want it to be too thick). Put the rub on the butt and let it sit in the fridge overnight. When you're ready to start cooking preheat the grill to 225-250°F. Let the pork butt cook until it has reached an internal temperature of around 170°F. At this point, it will have reached the "stall." Now is a good time to wrap it in foil and pour half a cup (you can use more depending on the size of your pork butt) of 100% pure apple juice in the foil. The apple juice will help steam the butt and cook it faster while adding moisture. Check the meat temperature and when it reaches 200°F take it out of the foil and put it back on the grill. You can add barbecue sauce while it's on the grill if you would like a thick bark (A thick crust on the meat). Let the temperature rise again to 205°F. At this point, the butt should feel soft and mushy. In other words, it's ready! If not, wrap in foil and let it go another hour with no liquid. After that remove the bone and start shredding. Use your favorite hamburger buns and garnish with coleslaw and dressing. This makes a boatload of food, so before diving into this recipe, make sure you have a party or gathering in mind!

Eve Got Adam's Spare Rib

Ingredients:

- Rub - Chupacabra Original Seasoning.
- Barbecue Sauce - Your choice! I recommend a 'Carolina Style' because that's my favorite.
- 2 Racks of Spare Ribs (Trust me, you'll want extra!)
- ½ Cup Yellow Mustard
- 1 Cup Apple Juice
- Aluminum Foil
- ½ Gallon Mustard Potato Salad
- 2 Cans (16 oz.) Baked Beans

Instructions:

My all-time favorite rib rub is Chupacabra Original Seasoning by 2 Gringo's. Its spicy, citrus-flavored rub goes well with any pork meat. That's why I use it on most of my BBQ smoked ribs.

Remove the membrane (aka Silver Skin) on the bone side of the ribs. This can be a slow process but it makes all the difference. I recommend watching a youtube video to get a good visual. The idea is to remove the silver skin because cooking it only makes the ribs tough and chewy.

Then, coat the ribs in yellow mustard to help the rub stick to the meat. Apply rub liberally and pat to help it stick to the mustard. Get the pit to 250°F. Put the ribs on the grill with the bone down and let them BBQ for two hours. When your timer goes off, remove the ribs and wrap them in foil. Add a little apple juice to the foil. Return to the grill for two more hours. After that remove the ribs from the foil and place them back on the grill. Start adding barbecue sauce every 15 minutes for the next 45 minutes. The BBQ sauce will caramelize into a delicious glaze. Remove after 45 minutes and slice to serve. I always serve ribs with a side of mustard potato salad and baked beans.

Smoked Hot Cock Wings

Ingredients:

- 2 Dozen Chicken Wings
- 1 Cup Tabasco Hot Sauce
- 1 Bottle Buffalo Wing Sauce
- 2 Tbsp. Unsalted Butter
- Special Sh*t Seasoning

Instructions:

When I cook, I cook a lot of food because leftover BBQ is impossible to beat. I recommend you buy no less than two dozen wings for this recipe, but don't hesitate to buy more! Put the chicken into a Ziploc bag and pour the ½ cup of Tabasco in, so that the chicken is coated well. Put the chicken into the ziplock bag and pour the ½ a cup of tabasco in so that all the chicken has some on it. Throw the bag in the fridge (in a bowl to catch any leaks) and let them marinate at least 12 hours. If you can wait 24 hours it'll be even tastier. After that, you should put a small amount of rub onto each piece of chicken. This is to help make the skin crispy. Get your grill going to 250°F and put the chicken on. Let the wings cook at that temperature for about an hour and a half. Then raise the temperature to 350-400°F and let them cook for another 15 minutes turning every 5 minutes. Take the chicken off and let it sit for about 10 minutes. During the final 5 minutes, melt the butter in a saucepan and add the remaining ½ cup of Tabasco and the Buffalo Wing Sauce. Bring it to a boil then remove it from the heat. Carefully drizzle the sauce on the cooked wings and serve. This recipe isn't for the faint of heart. The wings can be pretty spicy so warn your guests before digging in!

EH-gg, What's The Big 'Dillo?

These are a household favorite! They can be used as a side or main dish, depending on how many you make.

Ingredients:

- 24 Large Jalapeños
- 1 Pkg. Cream Cheese
- 1 Lb. Pan Sausage
- ½ Block Cheddar Cheese

▽ Instructions:

You need to start by cutting the jalapeños top off, removing the seeds, then put a mixture of cream cheese and cheddar where the seeds used to be. After that, take your pan sausage and form a ball around the jalapeño. Start up the grill and set it for 250°F. Let the "Eggs" smoke for about 2 hours. If you want them crispy then crank up the temperature for the last 20 minutes to somewhere closer to 350°F. Take off the grill and let sit for about 10 minutes. Enjoy!

I Wanna Grill A Spatchcock-Cock-Cock

The most important thing to remember about cooking a whole chicken is that the 'Spatchcock' style makes the chicken much easier to cook and minimizes cooking time!

Ingredients:

- 1 Whole Chicken
- Chicken Rub
- 3 Lemons (Juiced, and for garnish)

Instructions:

Below are instructions on how to cut the chicken.

- Place the chicken breast-side down, then adjust so the legs are pointing towards you.

- Next, use good kitchen scissors to cut along each side of the backbone to remove it. Be sure to cut through the rib bones, otherwise it will not lay flat.

- Flip it over and flatten the chicken by pressing down on the breastbone firmly. At this point the chicken should be lying symmetrically with each half the same size thickness.

- Lastly, secure the legs with two metal skewers and keep the bird flat. Run the skewers from the breast to the thigh to finish the job, and prepare for cooking.

Then it's time to rub the chicken. I use the rub from the hot chicken recipe. It's called "Rub Some Chicken" by BBQSPOT.COM. I highly recommend it if you want something quick and easy. Take the rubbed chicken and put it on the grill at 250°F for roughly 3 hours. Check the temperature and once it reaches around 185°F it's time to take it off the grill. If it gets up to 200°F it may be a little dry, but don't stress if its a little overcooked, it'll still taste great! Finally, juice the lemons on top and garnish with a few lemon wedges. Now, it's time to feast!

The Tri-Tip Steaks Have Never Been Higher

- Heat a smoker to run at 250°F.

- Trim the steak of any silver skin/membrane on the surface using a filet knife. This step isn't essential, but here's why you want to do it: unlike fat, which renders during cooking, silver skin doesn't break down and can result in a chewier bite.

- Season well with salt and pepper, then place into the smoker. If you have one, insert a probe to monitor temperature. If you don't have a probe device, use a meat thermometer to start checking the internal temperature at about 1.5 hours.

- Once the internal temperature at the thickest part reaches 130-135°F, remove the meat from the smoker and wrap tightly in foil or butchers paper. Allow it to rest for 20 minutes.

If you have some patience you won't be disappointed in the green Romesco sauce below. Trust me, it's worth it!

Ingredients:

- 1 Medium Green Bell Pepper, Cored and Cut into 2-inch Pieces
- 1 Large Poblano Chile, Stemmed and Cut into 2-inch Pieces
- 2 Garlic Cloves, Halved and Peeled
- 1 Tbsp. Extra-Virgin Olive Oil
- Salt
- Freshly Ground Black Pepper
- ½ Cup Raw Slivered Almonds
- ½ Cup Cilantro Leaves
- 1 Tsp. Sherry Vinegar
- ½ Cup Water

Instructions:

Preheat the oven to 400°F. On a baking sheet, toss the bell pepper, poblano and garlic with the oil; season with salt and pepper. Roast for 25 minutes, until softened. Scatter the almonds on top and roast for 8 minutes, until lightly golden. Let cool slightly, then transfer to a food processor with the cilantro, vinegar, and water; process to a chunky purée. Season the Romesco with salt and pepper and serve.

Texas Smokes Ribs Better

Ingredients:

- Kosher Salt, to taste
- Ground Pepper, to taste
- 1 Large Rack Beef Ribs
- ½ - 1 Cup Barbecue Sauce

This is easily my all-time favorite BBQ to cook! All you need is Kosher salt and ground pepper for a rub. I promise you despite the simple rub, this will knock your socks off. Unfortunately, it's hard for consumers to find beef ribs. Just be aware that some of these ribs are bigger than others. The bigger ones will take a longer time to cook because of their size.

Instructions:

Heat the grill to about 275°F, put the rubbed ribs on the grill and cook to around 205-210°F. For a big rack of ribs, this could take up to 6 hours while a smaller rack could be done in 3, so get that thermometer ready! Slather in the barbecue sauce with about 15 minutes to spare to really take the ribs to a whole new LEVEL!

Tender BBQ Bangers

Every time I tell somebody about this recipe... I get strange looks. Trust me, it is worth trying and I can guarantee it won't be the last time you make this!

Ingredients:

- 1-2 (16 oz.) Sausage Links, of your choice!
- Sea Salt (Add to water)
- 3 Cups Boiling Water
  (3 Cups for every 16 oz. of Sausage)

Instructions:

Preheat the grill to 375°F. Bring a pan or large pot to boil with the water and sea salt, then add the sausage in for about 10 minutes. Remove sausage from the water and take it to the grill for 15-20 minutes, rotating halfway through. Once they are done, that's it! Serve it straight or cut it up to enjoy!

Now, you're probably wondering why does sausage need to be boiled? Well, by boiling the sausage you can be sure of two things; 1) The sausage will stay moist, and 2) It will cook it evenly and completely. Throwing it on the grill adds that spark of flavor, but it can be ready to eat just after boiling.

Cock Swings

Ingredients:

- 4-6 Chicken Breast Filets (Boneless), Cut into 3-inch Slivers
- 8-12 Jalapeños, Halved
- 1 Pkg. (8 oz.) Cream Cheese
- 1 Pack Bacon (Recommended: Maple)

Instructions:

Here is yet another bacon-wrapped treasure! Cut the jalapeños in half, remove the seeds and veins, then add the cream cheese. Next, put a chicken sliver over the cream cheese and tightly wrap it all up in bacon! Use a toothpick to keep the bacon from sliding around, if necessary. Crank the grill up to 350°F and cook for 30 minutes minimum while turning every 5 minutes. Once the bacon has gotten crispy on all sides, remove it and enjoy!

Smoke 'Em In The Sockeye

:: Ingredients:

- 3-4 (6 oz.) Sockeye Salmon Fillets, With Skin
- Lemons, for Garnish
- Parsley, for Garnish
- 2 Tbsp. Dry Mix (Garlic Powder, Thyme, Onion Powder, Paprika, Sea Salt, and Black Pepper)

▼ Instructions:

I'm not going to lie and say that Salmon is my favorite dish on the grill, but for salmon lovers, and even some naysayers this dish may be the one to change your mind about grilled salmon. First, you'll want to generously season all sides of the salmon with the dry mix.

Once the salmon is seasoned, you'll want to prepare it by wrapping each fillet in saran wrap (skin-side up) and refrigerating them for half a day (10-12 hours). The effort might be why I don't cook salmon as often, but trust the process and you will be happy with the dish!

Next, remove the wrapped fillets from the fridge and let sit for approx. 1 hour, so that is becomes room temperature. Then place on a smoker at 160-170°F for approximately 6 hours. Do your best not to overcook the fish or it will become quite dry.

I use the fork test to see when my salmon is done. To do so, you should be able to gently use a fork to get the salmon meat to separate from the skin.

Once removed, let it sit in foil with the juice of a lemon. Top with lemon slices and parsley for garnish. Enjoy!

Porky's Potbelly On The Pit

:: Ingredients:

- 2.5-3 lbs. Pork Belly
- ½ Cup Brown Sugar
- ¼ Cup Kosher Salt
- 1 Tbsp. Freshly Ground Black Pepper
- 1 Tsp. Garlic Powder
- 1 Tbsp. Cayenne Pepper
- 1 Cup Barbecue Sauce
  (Recommended: 'Carolina Style')

▼ Instructions:

Cut the fat from the bottom of the pork belly. Trust me, there is already enough fat to go around on this cut of meat. Then cut the meat into 1-inch to 1 ½-inch cubes. Rub liberally then put on the grill at around 250-275°F. Let it cook for roughly 3 hours or until you're happy with the bark. Place the pork belly into an aluminum pan and fill with your favorite BBQ sauce. I use a sweet tangy Carolina style BBQ sauce with pork belly. When you remove it, allow it to rest for at least 20 minutes. After it's cooled a bit, cut it up and get to eatin'!

Sweet & Tangy Meatsicles

Ingredients:

- 1 Rack Baby Back Ribs
- 1 Tbsp. Dijon Mustard
- 1 Cup Apple Juice
- Aluminum Foil
- Pork Rub (Recommended: TexJoy Butt and Tickler Rub)
- ½-1 Cup Barbecue Sauce (Recommended: 'Carolina Style')

Instructions:

To begin, remove the membrane from the underside of the ribs before adding a small amount of mustard to the meat. Use the mustard to help the rub stick. After rubbing down the meat you can put the ribs on the grill and use the 2-2-1 method of rib cooking. Which means cook at 250°F for 2 hours, then wrap the ribs in foil and add apple juice. Cook for another 2 hours in the foil. Then remove the ribs from the foil and go 1 more hour. Apply BBQ sauce every 10 minutes for the final 30 minutes of cooking. This will make the BBQ sauce stick to the ribs and add a lot of extra flavor. Try not to go overboard on the sauce, but it honestly can't hurt!

The Name's Rib. Prime Rib.

Ingredients:

- 4 Bone-in Prime Rib Roast (Approx. 8 lbs.)
- 3 Tbsp. Dijon Mustard
- 2 Tbsp. Worcestershire Sauce
- 4 Cloves Garlic (mashed to a paste)
- 2 Tsp. Dried Thyme
- 2 Tsp. Dried Rosemary
- Horseradish
- Kosher Salt and Black Pepper

Instructions:

In a small bowl, whisk together the Dijon mustard, Worcestershire sauce, garlic, thyme, rosemary, salt and pepper. If the dried rosemary needles are long, finely chop them before adding.

Then, coat the Prime Rib in the mustard mixture. When you're ready to cook, heat the grill to 250°F and put the rib on. Let it cook roughly 2 hours before checking the temperature. Once the prime rib reaches 125-130°F degrees for Rare or 135°F for Medium-Rare, then take it off the grill. - Do NOT go past that! Serve with the horseradish and enjoy your hard work!

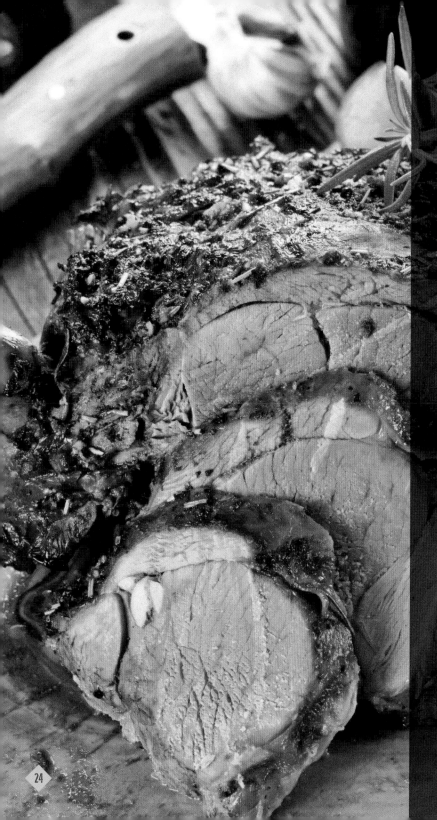

Ewe Sure Can Smoke 'Em

Ingredients:

- 1 Leg of Lamb, Aitchbone Removed, Fat Trimmed to ¼ Inch Thick and Tied
- 1 Bulb of Garlic, Chopped
- 2 Tbsp. Kosher Salt
- 2 Tbsp. Fresh Rosemary, Chopped
- 1 ½ Tsp. Fresh Ground Black Pepper
- ¼ Cup Dry Red Wine or Beef Broth
- ¼ Cup Olive Oil
- 1 Cube Beef Bouillon (Made into a broth)

▼ Instructions:

Combine the salt, pepper, and rosemary into a bowl. Rub the leg in olive oil to make sure it has a good coat to help the dry ingredients stick. Using kitchen scissors, make small incisions about 1/3-inch deep. Heat a skillet to medium heat and sauté the chopped garlic for about 10 minutes. Next, take the dry ingredients and sautéed garlic and rub generously on the leg. Set the smoker to 200°F and smoke the lamb for about a half an hour. Then, crank up the fire and get the temperature up to 350°F and let it cook for about 45-90 minutes, or until it reaches an internal temperature of 135°F. Remove the lamb and let it rest for 10 minutes. Enjoy, it's ready to eat!

Smokin' Karate Pigs

Ingredients:

- 4-6 (2-Inch) Thick Cut Pork Chops
- 1 Tbsp. Salt
- 2 Tbsp. White Pepper
- 1 Tbsp. Red Paprika
- 1 Tbsp. Onion Powder
- 1 Tbsp. Garlic Powder
- Olive Oil
- ½ Tsp. Cayenne Pepper (Optional, for added heat)

Instructions:

Start by mixing the salt, white pepper, onion, cayenne, garlic powder, and paprika in a bowl. Remove the pork chops from the package and apply the rub. After that, fire up your grill and get it to 250°F. If you want the chops to be a little crispy, then you should sear them on a cast iron skillet after or before smoking. I believe that flavor is enhanced if you sear them after smoking. They should be done cooking after 75-85 minutes on the smoker, or until they reach an internal temperature of 145-155°F. Take them off the grill and enjoy after letting them rest 10 minutes. Dig in!

Roast Malone Gets Smoked

Ingredients:

- 1 Chuck Roast (3-4 lbs.)
- 2 Tbsp. Kosher Salt
- 2 Tbsp. Coarse Black Pepper
- 2 Tbsp. Garlic Powder
- 1 Chuck roast 3-4 pounds
- 1 White Onion, Sliced
- 3 Cups Beef Stock
  (Divided Use)

▼ Instructions:

Combine the salt, pepper, and garlic powder in a bowl and rub onto the roast. Allow the roast to rest in the fridge, covered, for 12 hours. Set the smoker for 225°F and pour 1 cup of the beef stock into a spray mist bottle. Let it cook for 3 hours then crank it up to 250°F. Once you do that, slice the onions into strips and put them into a disposable aluminum pan. Add the remaining 2 cups of beef stock as well. Then add the Roast into the aluminum pan on top of the onions. This will make a delicious Au Jus. After another 3 hours, check the temperature of the meat. When it reaches 200°F, it is ready! Remove the roast and shred it with a fork, then use a ladle to cover it in the Au Jus and enjoy!

Smoked Turkey Boob

Ingredients:

- 1.5 Lb. Boneless, Skinless Turkey Breast
- 2 Cups Lemon-Lime Soda
- 1 Cup Low-Sodium Soy Sauce
- ½ Cup Canola Oil
- 1 Tbsp. Creamy Horseradish Sauce
- 1 Tbsp. Garlic Powder
- Salt and Pepper, to taste

Instructions:

Combine all the ingredients besides the turkey into a Ziploc bag and shake it like you mean it! Add the turkey and let it marinate in the fridge for at least 6 hours. Heat your smoker to 225°F and put the marinated turkey onto the grill. Place the marinade you used into an aluminum pan and put that onto the grill as well. Let it cook for 2 hours or until it reaches 150°F, then put the turkey into the marinade on the grill. Next, increase the temperature of the grill as high as it can go. However, do not exceed 700°F. Once it reaches that temperature, remove the breasts and put them on the grill for about 3 minutes on each side or until the skin is crispy. Remove the breast at an internal temperature 160-170°F and cut into thin slices. Get ready to lick your fingers!

This Tenderloin Is Bacon Me Crazy

Ingredients:

- 1 Pack Bacon
- 1 Pork Tenderloin
- 4 Tbsp. Dijon Mustard
- 2 Tbsp. Minced Parsley
- 2 Tbsp. Minced Tarragon
- ¼ Tbsp. Kosher Salt
- ¼ Tbsp. Brown Pepper
- ¼ Cup Vegetable Oil
- Wood Skewers (Optional)

Instructions:

Take the tenderloin and rub it with the vegetable oil. Mix the mustard, parsley, tarragon, salt, and pepper and rub it into the tenderloin. Wrap the bacon around the tenderloin and secure with skewers. Heat the grill to 375°F, put the wrapped tenderloin on the grill and turn every 10 minutes. After 30 minutes start checking the internal temperature. Once it reaches 165°F, it is done. This could take an extra 5-30 minutes. Dig in!

Clod You Beef Any Tastier?

Ingredients:

- 1 Beef Clod Roast (8-10 oz.)
- 4 Tbsp. Kosher Salt
- 4 Tbsp. Ground Pepper
- ½ Tsp. Paprika
- ½ Tsp. Sugar
- ½ Tsp. Garlic Powder
- ½ Tsp. Onion Powder

Instructions:

Rub the beef clod with salt, pepper, garlic, ground onion, paprika, and sugar. Place in the refrigerator and allow it to marinate for at least 24 hours. Heat the pit to 225°F, then place the clod into the smoker. Check the temperature until it reaches 175°F. It should take an hour per pound of meat for it to cook. Since beef clod is so heavy it could take 20+ hours to get it to the target temperature. If you're impatient or in a hurry, you can wrap the clod in foil after 10 hours to speed up the process. After it reaches the target temperature, it is ready to eat! Enjoy!

Not Your Average Mutton Bustin'

⁝ Ingredients:

- 2 Racks Sheep Ribs
- ½ Cup Kosher Salt
- ½ Cup Ground Pepper
- ⅓ Cup Barbecue Sauce (Optional for Dip)

▼ Instructions:

Rub the sheep ribs generously with salt and pepper mixture. You will use the 3-2-1 method in the same manner as pork ribs. Put the ribs on the grill at 250°F and let them cook for 3 hours. Then after that wrap the ribs in foil. Let them sit on the grill for another 2 hours, then remove them and let them cook for another hour. Once they are finished, use your favorite barbecue sauce as the dip and enjoy!

Smokin' Hot Jon Hamm

Glaze Ingredients:

- 2 Sticks Salted Butter
- 1 ½ Cup Dark Brown Sugar
- ½ Cup Pure Maple Syrup
- ⅓ Cup Apple Cider
- ¼ Cup Spiced Rum
- 1 Tsp. Ground Cinnamon

Rub Ingredients:

- 1 ½ Cups Smoked Paprika
- ½ Cup Sugar
- ¼ Cup Onion Powder
- 1 Tsp. Nutmeg

Instructions:

Season the ham with the rub recipe, then let it chill overnight in the refrigerator. Remove it in the morning and heat the grill to 250°F. Put the ham on and let it cook for 3 hours. Next, add the glaze recipe into an aluminum pan and put it on the grill for half an hour. Take the glaze out and baste the ham every 5 minutes for 15 minutes. Lastly, take the ham off the grill and pour the rest of the glaze over the ham. Cut and serve immediately. Get ready to make everyone happy with this recipe!

Smoked Aphrodisiacs

Ingredients:

- 50 Oysters in the Shell, Medium-sized
- ¼ Cup Expeller Pressed Olive Oil (Optional Substitutes: Walnut or Hazelnut Oil)
- ¾ Cup Water
- 1 ½ Cups White Wine

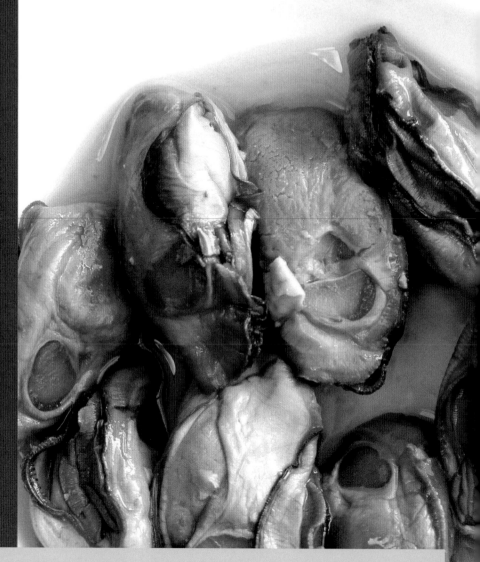

Instructions:

To begin, pour the white wine and water into a pot and bring it to a boil. Rinse the oysters in cold water and remove any debris, then add the oysters to the boiling pot of water. After a few minutes, the oysters will open and you can remove them from the pot. Using a sharp knife, separate the oyster from the shell, but leave the meat in the shell with the connective tissue (This just makes it easier to eat later on). Heat your smoker to 150°F and place the oysters on the pit for about an hour and a half. Once they are fully cooked, toss them in the oil, or choice of sauce, and enjoy!

Risk It For The Hot Brisket

Rub Ingredients:

- ¼ Cup Paprika
- ¼ Cup Chili Powder
- ¼ Cup Black Pepper
- ¼ Cup Kosher Salt
- ¼ Cup Onion Powder
- ¼ Cup Garlic Powder

Baste Ingredients:

- One Bottle Beer
- 2 Tbsp. Olive Oil
- 1 Tbsp. Ground Cayenne Pepper
- 1 Tbsp. Black Pepper

Instructions:

Rub the brisket thoroughly with the rub above. Let the brisket sit in the fridge for at least 12 hours. Set up the grill for 225-250°F and put the brisket on, fat side up. After it has cooked for 6 hours, begin basting it. Check the temperature every 30-60 minutes and baste while you check. Once the internal temperature reaches 205°F it will be close to done. Let it sit there for roughly 30 minutes without basting. Wrap it in foil, then a towel, and place it into a cooler. It will allow the fats to keep rendering without risk of burning the outside. Slice and serve warm with your favorite BBQ sauce.

Smokey Sweet Fingerlickin' Ribs

Ingredients:

- 2 (5 Lb. Racks) . Baby Back Pork Ribs
- ¼ Cup Salt
- ¼ Cup White Sugar
- ¼ Cup Brown Sugar
- 2 Tbsp. Ground Black Pepper
- 2 Tbsp. Ground White Pepper
- 3 Tbsp. Onion Powder
- 2 Tbsp. Garlic Powder
- 1 Tbsp. Chili Powder
- 1 Tbsp. Ground Paprika
- 1 ½ Tbsp. Ground Cumin
- 1 ½ Cups Apple Cider
- ½ Cup BBQ Sauce (Recommended: Sweet Baby Ray's)

Instructions:

First, remove the silver skin from the rib side of the ribs. These ribs are going to be tender, so don't let this membrane ruin the dish!

Use 2 Tbsps. of brown sugar, barbecue sauce, and the ¼ cup of apple cider and combine them into a mixing cup to blend. After that, take the rest of the dry ingredients and combine everything in the cup. Rub thoroughly onto the ribs. Set the grill to 270°F and put the ribs on! Let them cook for 2 hours, then remove. Place the ribs onto foil with the remaining apple cider and let them go for 90 minutes from there. Remove the foil and cook for another 60-75 minutes. Take them off the grill, cut up and serve. Get ready to start eating!

Pho King Best Spicy Ribs!

Ingredients:

- 1 Rack Baby Back Ribs
- 3 Tbsp. Packed Brown Sugar
- 2 Tbsp. Paprika
- 3 Tbsp. Chili Powder
- 3 Tbsp. Ground Cumin
- 3 Tbsp. Garlic Powder
- 1 Tbsp. Salt

Glaze Ingredients:

- 1 Cup Low-Sodium Soy Sauce
- 1 Cup Brown Sugar
- ½ Cup Ketchup
- ¼ Cup Lemon Juice

▼ Instructions:

Preheat your grill to 325-350°F. Combine rub ingredients into a bowl, and mix them thoroughly. Remove the membrane (silver skin) on the bone side of the ribs. Pat the ribs dry with a paper towel and place them on foil. Apply the rub liberally and wrap the the foil around the ribs. Put them on the grill, bone-side down and grill for an hour. Then take the glaze ingredients and rub it on the ribs. Put them back on the grill for 15 minutes and then remove. Let them rest for 10 minutes before serving. Enioy!

This Brisket Just Yee'd It's Last Haw

Ingredients:

- Beef Brisket (Approx. 1-1.6Lbs.)
- ⅓ Cup Thick Ground Pepper
- ⅓ Cup Kosher Salt

Instructions:

The key to good brisket is a low and slow cooking method. Texas-style barbecue uses a simple rub of salt and pepper. If you cook it right, you won't even need barbecue sauce! Let the flavor of the meat do the talking!

Set the pit to 225-250°F and put the rubbed brisket on, with the fat facing the direction of the heat. (i.e. If your heat is coming from coals below the meat, put the fat cap down. If you're using an offset smoker, then it can be placed up. If you're thinking, "Why wouldn't I want the fat facing up so it can soak the meat?" - Trust me, it has been shown that the fat will not make the meat more juicy.)

So, how long will it take to cook? The short answer is a while. A good general rule of thumb is that it will take about 1.5 hours for every lb. of brisket you're cooking. My general gameplan is once the brisket reaches 190°F, you should let it go for another hour and then take it out. The reason is that the fat starts to render around 185°F, and will need time. Once that's over, remove the brisket and let it sit for 30 minutes in foil. Then cut it up and eat!

Smokin' Half a Cock

Ingredients:

- 1 Whole Chicken, Cut Into Half
- 1 Tsp. Paprika
- ¼ Cup. Brown Sugar
- 1 Tsp. Salt
- 2 Tsp. Garlic Powder
- 1 Tsp. Garlic Salt
- 2 Tsp. Black Pepper
- ½ Tsp. Crushed Red Pepper Flakes
- ½ Tsp. Dried Thyme
- ½ Tsp. Dried Oregano

Instructions:

Mix dry ingredients into a bowl to create the rub. Preheat your grill to 300°F. Once you cover the entire chicken in the rub, cover and let it marinate in the fridge for 30 minutes. This will help the rub stick to the slippery chicken skin. Add wood chips or chunks to the coals to add a dynamic smokey flavor!

Right after you add the chips, put the meat on the grill. Flip the chicken twice over the course of 1 hour. If you can increase the heat of your grill, do so for the last 10 minutes to help crisp the skin. It will be done once the internal temperature reaches 165°F. Remove from heat, slice around the bones and enjoy!

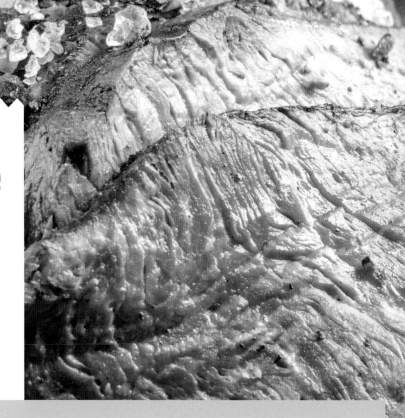

Too Much At Steak, We Need To Bison Time

Ingredients:

- 4 (1-inch) Bison Ribeyes
- 1 Tbsp. Kosher Salt
- 2 Tbsp. Coarse Ground Black Pepper
- 1 Tsp. Garlic Salt
- 1 Tsp. Onion Powder
- 2 Tbsp. Grapeseed Oil

Instructions:

I'm a firm believer that there a just a few keys to making perfect steaks.

1. Let the meat reach room temperature before you throw it on the grill.

2. Let the flame hit the steak. (Don't fear the flame!)

3. Cook it Rare or Medium-Rare at most! The leaner the meat, the closer to Rare you should cook it to prevent toughness. Follow these simple steps and you can throw almost anything on your steak, and it'll still turn out like a 5-star Chef cooked it. Onto the recipe!

Combine the dry ingredients in a small mixing bowl and mix. Apply the grapeseed oil to both sides of the bison and pat your meat down with the dry rub. I prefer using an infrared burner when cooking my steaks because it really chars the outside, while not overcooking the inside. I cook this way rather than closing the lid to create a convection heating environment. Since the bison is so lean, it shouldn't drip much fat and cause a flare up, but keep in mind that the oil could. Remember, small flare ups are okay, but always make sure to keep an eye on it to avoid it getting out of control. While cooking, flip the steak 4-5 times to ensure even cooking and pull the meat off once it reaches 125°F. This shouldn't take more than 2-3 minutes per side. Lastly, allow the meat to rest on a serving platter for about 5 minutes before slicing it thinly. Now you're ready to enjoy yourself a tender bison steak!

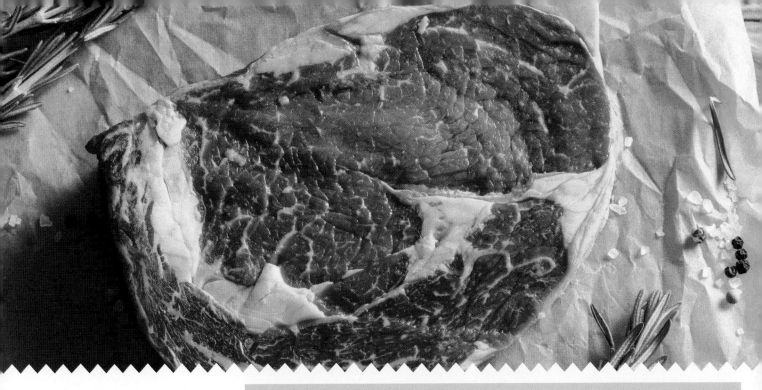

Boujee Ribeye

Ingredients:

- 4 (1-inch) Ribeye Steaks
- Vacuum Sealer or 2 1-Gallon Ziploc Bags
- Fresh Thyme
- Rock Salt
- Course Ground Black Pepper
- 4 Garlic Cloves, Chopped
- 4 Tbsp. Grapeseed Oil
- 1 Tbsp. Unsalted Butter

▼ Instructions:

This is one of my favorite ways to cook in the winter or on a rainy day. When you don't have access to a grill or want to spend some quality time indoors, this is a go-to recipe that will have your friends and family raving! To begin, fill a large pot with water and set up your Sous Vide, according the directions included with it. Set the temperature to 122°F and preheat the water. Coat the steaks in Grapeseed oil, salt, fresh thyme, black pepper, and chopped garlic. Vacuum seal your steaks and put them into the pot. Set the timer for an hour and prepare your tastebuds!

The Sous Vide will cook your meat to perfection, but don't be fooled, it will not look like a steakhouse steak when you pull it out of the water. To me, it actually doesn't look nearly as good as it smells, but that won't last long. Heat your skillet with a pad of butter on it, and wait until it's starting to smoke. (You may want your vent on and a window/door open before the next step). Throw your meat on the skillet and let it sizzle for about 1 minute on each side. Remember, that you are really just adding the sear to the steak because it's already cooked perfectly through. Allow the meat to rest for about 5 minutes before slicing. I'm not gonna lie, you may wonder why you even own a grill after trying this Boujee Steak!

Instructions:

I'm not listing these recipes in any particular order, but if I were, this may be my #1! If you're an experienced griller/smoker you'll know ways to cheat this recipe, but prime rib is by far my favorite meat to eat, so I don't mind taking my time to get this one right.

Many will tell you to buy the bone-in, but I can assure you that whether you buy a choice cut or prime cut, bone-in or bone-out, you'll love this recipe! However, because this is one since this is one of the pricier cuts, I recommend starting with a cheaper cut until you perfect it. Regardless, they will all turn out great if you follow this recipe step-by-step!

Rotisserie the PR on indirect heat over an open flame. This is more about the smoke and creating a crust on the PR than it is cooking it to a perfect internal temperature. You'll only want to do the rotisserie for about 20 minutes. It's a decent amount of work to get the smoke flavor, but trust the process.

While the meat is on the rotisserie, preheat your oven to 275°F. Remove the PR after 20 minutes, place in a roasting pan, and put it in the oven for about 1-2 hours, or until the internal temperature reaches 125°F.

While the meat is roasting in the oven, you are ready to prepare the Horseradish Sauce. Start by combining the horseradish, sour cream, Worcestershire, and spicy mustard in a bowl. Mix well and refrigerate until you are to serve the meat. Warning: This sauce will bring the heat on quickly, but should dissipate just as fast!

Remove the meat from the oven and allow it to rest for 30 minutes. YES, 30 Minutes! Slice and serve on hawaiian rolls with a dollop of horseradish sauce. You're welcome.

Winston Church-Grill, Prime Rib Of Steaks

Ingredients:

- 1 Ribeye End (4-6 Lb.)
- 6 Garlic Cloves, Chopped
- Whole Peppercorn
- Rock Salt
- 1 Tsp. Fresh Rosemary
- 1 Tsp. Fresh Thyme
- ¼ Cup Olive Oil

Horseradish Sauce:

- 1 Tbsp. Horseradish
- 12 oz. Sour Cream
- 1 Tbsp. Worcestershire Sauce
- 1 Tsp. Spicy Mustard

Going Vegan Is A Big Misteak!

Ingredients:

- 2 (¾-inch) Porterhouse Steaks
- Dry Steak Seasoning
- 2 Tsp. Kosher Salt
- 2 Tbsp. Coarse Black Pepper
- 2 Tbsp. Coffee Grounds
- 1 Tsp. Grapeseed Oil

Garlic Butter Sauce:

- 4 Tbsp. Unsalted Butter
- 1 Head of Garlic
- 1 Tsp. Worcestershire Sauce
- ½ Tsp. Spicy Yellow Mustard
- ½ Tsp. Kosher Salt
- 1 Tbsp. Olive Oil

Instructions:

Begin by coating your Porterhouse steaks in the Grapeseed oil. This is my favorite oil to grill at high temperatures with because of it's high smoke point and neutral flavor. Next, combine the dry ingredients for the steak rub and generously season the steaks.

Garlic Butter: Start by sauteing your unpeeled garlic in olive oil at medium-high heat. Stir continuously, until you have a nice brown wrapper around each clove of garlic, approx. 5-7 minutes. Peel the warm garlic and combine with the butter, Worcestershire sauce, salt, and mustard. Use a fork to mash the garlic into the butter and other ingredients. Stir until the garlic only exists in small pieces. Cover and place in the refrigerator to firm.

Grilling Your Steaks: Be sure to allow your steaks to rest for approximately 30 minutes prior to grilling so that they are at room temperature. Heat your grill to a minimum of 450°F, preferably up to 600°F. Sear your steaks for 1 ½ minutes on each side and then transition to a grill that is 350°F. Cook for approximately 2 minutes further on each side. *(Authors note - I personally use a searing burner which allows me to also have my pit at 350°F. The transition is much easier.)*

Put a dollop of refrigerated garlic butter on the steak, as soon as you take them off the grill. Allow them to rest for 5 minutes before serving. Enjoy this medley of flavor and be prepared to share your garlic butter recipe with the whole family!

Wicked Good Lobstah Mac

Ingredients:

- 1-2 Lb. Lobster
- 1 Pkg. Macaroni (8-12 Ounces)
- ½ Cup Bread Crumbs
- 16 Oz. Sharp Cheddar, Shredded
- 4 Tbsp. Unsalted Butter
- 8 Oz. Smoked Gouda
- 8 Oz. Whole Milk or Cream
- Seafood Seasoning (Recommended: Old Bay)
- Salt and Black Pepper, to Taste
- ½ Tbsp. Parsley

Instructions:

This savory dish is one of my favorites, but usually saved for special occasions. Start by getting your grill to 400°F. Boil your pasta until it is still slightly firm. You'll be grilling it so if you overcook it in boiling water, it may begin to disintegrate on the pit. Cut up and mix the cheeses in a bowl along with the butter, milk, seafood seasoning, salt, pepper, and lobster. Once your pasta is strained but still warm, combine all ingredients, except the bread crumbs in the mixing bowl. Spoon mixture into a large ceramic baking dish carefully, so that you don't break up the pasta. Add the bread crumbs on top. Place the dish on indirect heat for 25-30 minutes. Once the cheese begins to bubble through the bread crumbs and the bread crumbs begin to turn brown, you'll know the dish is done! Sprinkle with parsley for garnish, serve warm and enjoy!

Bacon Got Jalapeño Business

Ingredients:

- 24 Jalapeño Peppers, Halved
- 2 Pkgs. (8 Oz.) Cream Cheese
- 1 Pkg. Imitation Crab Meat
  (Or real crab meat, if you're boujee)
- 12 Oz. Sour Cream
- 1 Yellow Onion, Diced
- 24 Slices Bacon
- Seasoning Salt
  (Recommended: Sriracha)
- Toothpicks

Instructions:

Begin by cutting the jalapeños in half, deveining and deseeding with a spoon.

Stuffing: Allow cream cheese to soften in a bowl before completing the next step. Combine sour cream, cream cheese, chopped crab meat and finely diced onions in a bowl and mix thoroughly. Use a small spoon to stuff each jalapeño cavity with the crab concoction (you can enjoy leftover stuffing with Fritos).

Next, carefully wrap each jalapeño with a slice of raw bacon and secure with toothpicks. Place each wrapped jalapeño on the foil, until all of them are ready to grill! Grill for approx. 1 ½ hours at 250°F. Remember to remove the toothpicks before enjoying your tasty poppers!

Kick Some Asparag-ASS!

Ingredients:

- 2 Lbs. Asparagus
- 2 Tsp. White Pepper
- 2 Tsp. Kosher Salt
- 4 Cloves Garlic, Chopped
- 1 Pkg. Shredded Parmesan Cheese
- 4 Tbsp. Olive Oil

Instructions:

To begin, break the asparagus stems so you don't end up with stringy ends. If you don't know what I'm talking about, this recipe may not be for you. Coat the asparagus stems in olive oil. Toss generously. Lay asparagus in single layer on foil platter. Evenly distribute chopped garlic, white pepper, and Kosher salt. Grill asparagus on indirect heat on foil platter at 350°F for approximately 30 minutes. Toss occasionally. At 25 minutes, generously sprinkle parmesan cheese to coat the asparagus. Close lid and grill for remaining 5 minutes. Serve warm. This recipe pairs great with the Porterhouse Steak recipe, or be a savage and just eat the greens!

Rootin' Tootin' Grilled Veggies

Ingredients:

- 1 Large Yellow Squash
- 1 Large Zucchini
- 2 Large Carrots
- 1 Yellow or Red Bell Pepper
- 1 Lb. Asparagus
- ¼ Cup Olive Oil
- 1 Tbsp. Garlic Salt
- 1 Tsp. Coarse Ground Black Pepper
- 1 Tsp. Cumin
- 1 Small Lemon

Instructions:

Chop the veggies into ¼-inch slivers. Remove seeds and veins as needed from the peppers. Be mindful to keep chopped veggies to similar sizes in order to cook evenly. In a large bowl coat the veggies with olive oil, garlic salt, cumin, and pepper. Toss veggies into foil platter. Squeeze half a lemon over the veggies and then toss other half into foil. Grill at 350°F on indirect heat for 35 minutes. Grill directly on the grill to add another layer of flavor, but be careful not to let them fall through the grates. Toss occasionally to prevent sticking. Serve hot or cold. Pairs well with just about EVERYTHING!

Quit Cryin', It's Just An Onion!

∵ Ingredients:

- 2 Large Yellow Onions
- 6 Slices Bacon
- 1 Stick Butter
- ¼ Cup Lowry's Seasoning Salt

▼ Instructions:

Begin by peeling the onion to remove skin. Slice each onion 3 to 4 times towards root without slicing through entire onion. Place semi-sliced onion on large foil sheet; cut up half stick of butter and insert inside. Cover with seasoning salt. Wrap 3 slices of bacon around the top of the onion towards the bottom, then use the remaining 3 slices of bacon to wrap from the bottom to the top, and fold the foil around the entire onion. Place upright on grill. Cook on indirect heat at 250°F for 2 ½ hours. Once onion is ready to eat, pour into bowl and serve hot.

Drink Like Don Draper

:: *Ingredients & Supplies:*

- 2 Oz. Bourbon, of your Choice
- Angostura Bitters
- 1 Large Ice Cube
- Orange and Lemon Peels
- 8-10" Hickory Plank of Wood (flat)
- Whiskey Glass
- Lighter

I love a good Old Fashioned, but this recipe takes them to new heights! You'll need to find a hickory plank - my recommendation, a Pecan or Oak plank would work well, but I'd steer clear of Cedar as it can be too strong. Start by organizing your ingredients nearby. This doesn't take long once the board starts burning so you'll want to be ready. Using a knife or fork, chip away a small quarter size section in the board. You'll want to create just a few shavings. Next, light the shavings with the lighter and place the whiskey glass over it face down. Any fire that was create will quickly be put out (no oxygen to feed it), but you will get smoke filling the glass. Allow the glass to sit there for 1 minute. When you pull it off the board, add the large ice cube, your whiskey, angostura bitters (to taste, but 4-6 dashes should do) and rub your orange/lemon peels around the rim of the glass. Stir and sip!

I must note that this recipe isn't smoke-infused because I find those way too time consuming, and honestly not all that delicious. This simple recipe gives you the smokiness via smell which translates to taste. Give it a shot and you won't be disappointed. Cheers!

Bean There, Grilled That

Ingredients:

- 1 Lb. Fresh Green Beans (be sure to remove the stems)
- 1 Dozen Fresh Cherry Tomatoes, Halved
- 4 Tbsp. Parmesan Cheese
- 1 Lemon
- 8 Oz. Mozzarella Cheese
- 4 Tbsp. Olive Oil
- Salt to Taste

▼ Instructions:

This dish can be super healthy if you don't add the cheese or if you have any issues with dairy. I recommend you try it with and without! Start by heating your pit to 350°F. In a large bowl combine the raw green beans, halved cherry tomatoes, lemon juice from one freshly squeezed lemon, lemon pepper, and olive oil. Mix thoroughly and move it to a ceramic dish for the grill. Place the dish on indirect heat for 25 minutes. Stir occasionally to keep the beans from sticking to the pan. At the 25 minute mark, sprinkle the mozzarella and parmesan cheeses across the top. Cook until the cheese has melted, approximately 10 more minutes. Once you've removed the dish from the pit, stir until everything is mixed again. Finish with salt to taste and enjoy!

I'm Green From
My Head To-ma-toes

Ingredients:

- 3 Green Tomatoes
- Salt & Pepper
- 1 Tsp. Parsley
- 1 Tsp. Basil
- Olive Oil

▼ Instructions:

A simple and delicious dish, if you can find green tomatoes! Cut the tomatoes into thin slivers, about ¼ to ⅓ inches thick. Cut them evenly, so they all cook at the same speed. Coat the slivers with olive oil and season them on both sides with the basil, salt and pepper. You'll want the pit around 350°F. Grill the tomatoes over direct heat for 4-6 minutes on each side. Once they gain their grill marks and soften a bit, remove them from the heat and place on a serving dish. Sprinkle the parsley flakes over the tomatoes and serve hot. This pairs great with any of the heavy meat dishes!

Grillin' Up
A Dr. Seuss
Book

✦ Ingredients:

- 4 Red or Black Drum Fillets (½ Skin-on)
- 2 Tbsp. Butter, Softened
- Blackened Seasoning

▼ Instructions:

If you're not currently a lover of fish, this simple recipe may just change your opinion. I grew up eating fried catfish, so venturing into grilled fish seemed silly at first because fried fish is impossible to beat. It wasn't until I stumbled upon this recipe that that was true (at least to me)!

Heat your grill to 350°F. Generously spread the butter on the flesh of the fish and coat it with blackened seasoning. Place the fish (skin-side down) over direct heat and close the lid. You can keep it closed for about 5 minutes, but be sure to keep an eye on it as the butter may cause a flare up. After 5 minutes you'll spend the remainder of the time cooking it with the lid open and the butter in hand. Keep the flesh moist by generously adding additional butter on the fish, every few minutes for the remainder of the cook. Depending on the size of the fish, you will cook it an additional 15-20 minutes. Be sure to test it in the thickest part before you pull it off the grill. It's a flaky, white fish so it should easily pull away from the skin when it is ready to eat. Melt a little butter on the side for a tasty dip. This dish pairs wonderfully with cajun rice and hushpuppies! Enjoy.

It's Not What It Looks Like! It's American Pie!

⠿ Ingredients:

- 1 ½ Cups Brown Sugar
- 6-8 Red Apples, Sliced
- 1 Stick Unsalted Butter
- 1 Tsp. Cinnamon
- ½ Tsp. Nutmeg
- 1 Box Yellow Cake Mix

▼ Instructions:

I'm not going to cover how to create hot coals or how to use a dutch oven. I'm going to make some assumptions here. If you don't know either, google is a great resource for this. It's super simple and if you've never used a dutch oven, you'll make a point to use it as often as possible after you try this recipe.

Start by placing your cut apples along the bottom of the oven in a single layer. Next, evenly distribute ⅔ of the brown sugar over the apples. Next, pour the box of yellow cake mix over the apples and brown sugar. Now, sprinkle the remaining brown sugar, cinnamon, and nutmeg over the top of the cake mix. No need to mix! Last, but not least, cut small squares from the stick of butter and place them on top. Cover with your lid and cook with 10-12 briquets underneath the oven and 10-15 on top. The cobbler shouldn't take more than 45 minutes to cook, but you should check it at the 30 minute mark just in case the briquettes are hotter than normal. Serve warm with vanilla ice cream. You're welcome.

Get To The Peach Cobblah!

:: Ingredients:

- 12-15 Fresh Peaches, Sliced (Frozen will work, too)
- 1 Tsp. Cinnamon
- ½ Tsp. Nutmeg
- 1 Stick Unsalted Butter
- 1 Cup Sugar
- 1 Box Yellow Cake Mix

▼ Instructions:

Since your a seasoned pro with the dutch oven now, I'll move directly to the recipe. In a large bowl mix the peaches and sugar. Pour this mixture into the oven and cover it with the yellow cake mix. Add pads of butter all around then sprinkle the cinnamon and nutmeg over that. Place 10-12 coals underneath and 10-15 on top. Cook for approximately 35 minutes but check at the 30 minute mark. When the cake mix is brown across the top and you can stick a toothpick through without bringing much back up, it's ready to serve. Serve warm with vanilla ice cream, and thank me later!

Don't Beef Stewpid, I'm The Grill Master

Ingredients:

- 1 Yellow Onion, Diced
- 1.5 Lbs Cut Stew Meat
- 1 (14.5 Oz.) Can Green Beans
- 1 (15.25 Oz.) Can Corn
- 1 (14.5 Oz.) Can Diced Tomatoes
- 1 Head of Garlic, Finely Diced
- 2 Large Potatoes (1-inch Chunks)
- 4 Large Carrots (1-inch Chunks)
- 2 Pkgs. McCormick's Stew Seasoning
- Beef Bouillon Cubes or Seasoning (1 Tsp. Per Cup of Water)
- 2 Tbsp. Grapeseed Oil

Instructions:

I used to make this with my father in the winter time. We always used whatever canned goods we had in the pantry at the time, but they tended to be what I mentioned in the ingredients above. I love to experiment, so feel free to throw something in that I didn't mention.

In a hot dutch oven, brown the meat in grapeseed oil. Once browned, add the chopped onions and finely diced garlic. Stir mixture until onions are translucent. Next, add your chopped veggies, canned green beans, corn, and diced tomatoes. Pour 2 cups of water at a time into the oven until it is almost completely covered. Should be about 8 cups. Next add 8 tsps. Beef bouillon and the 2 packets of stew seasoning and stir. Bring this to a boil. Once it boils remove the oven from the stove and place the lid on it. Add 15 briquettes underneath the oven and 15 on top. You'll cook this for 1.5-2 hours. You may occasionally need to replace briquettes as they lose their heat. When you can easily stick a fork through the carrot chunks then it is ready to eat. This is a super savory dish and perfect for the Fall or Winter seasons.

Sir Loin Chillin' In His Newcastle

Ingredients:

- 4 (12 Oz.) Sirloin Steaks
- Salt & Coarse Ground Black Pepper
- 4 Tbsp. Grapeseed Oil
- ⅔ Cup Chili Powder
- 1 Garlic Bulb, Chopped
- ½ Tsp. Red Pepper
- 2 Tbsp. Onion Powder
- 2 Tbsp. Cumin
- 6 Pack Newcastle Brown Ale
- 1 White Onion, Chopped
- 2 Jalapeños, Seeded & Diced
- 1 (14.5 Oz.) Diced Tomatoes
- 2 Cans Red Kidney Beans (Drained and Rinsed)

Instructions:

You'll need a large pot for this. I typically like to drink my beer, but trust me, it's worth the little extra expense for this recipe. (I'm more a Miller guy anyhow). Coat your steaks in grapeseed oil and cover with salt and coarse ground black pepper. Grill these over direct heat until they are cooked to medium. Allow them to rest for about 10 minutes then chop into ½-inch chunks. The real secret to this dish is the grill/burn marks you get on your steaks so don't be afraid of the flame. The flame is your friend! It adds a level of flavor you'll never get in chili anywhere else.

Once the steaks are chopped add all the ingredients remaining in a large pot. Begrudgingly pour your 6 Newcastles into the pot (no water needed, for now). Bring the pot to a boil, then lower the temperature to a simmer for the next hour. Add water if you feel it needs it. Your steaks will continue to cook down and eventually you'll be left with a chunky chili. It's over the top good. It's even better the second day. Man, I love chili! Some crazy people say you shouldn't eat chili with beans, but I'm not one of them. I like hearty meals and this is just that. Serve with crackers and shredded cheddar cheese and fresh onions. A dollop of sour cream won't hurt either!

Livin' Beef Fajita Loca!

Ingredients:

- 2 Lbs. Skirt Steak (peeled)
- 2 Cups Soy Sauce
- 1 Cup Olive Oil
- 1 Cup Steak Sauce (Lea and Perrins)
- 1 Cup of Water
- 1 Tbsp. Black Pepper
- 1 Tbsp. Garlic Powder
- 1 Tsp. Cumin
- 2 Tbsp. Seasoning Salt
- Tortillas and Fixings

Instructions:

Start this delicious dish by combining soy sauce, olive oil, water, and steak sauce in a large cup. Mix thoroughly, and coat your skirt steak. Allow it to marinate for about 15 minutes. Next, combine the pepper, garlic, cumin and seasoning salt. Place the skirt steak on a hot grill and cook for about 5-6 minutes per side. While grilling, generously sprinkle the dry seasoning on the skirt steak. Be sure to season both sides as it grills.

Remember to cut across the grain of the meat to make it easier to eat. Serve on warm tortillas with all the fixings!

Brewski Cock With Your Broski

Ingredients:

- 2 Whole Chickens
- ⅓ Cup Thyme
- 2 Tbsp. Rosemary
- 4 Tbsp. Olive Oil
- 2 Tbsp. Seasoning Salt
- 2 Cans Beer of your choice

Instructions:

This is an incredibly simple recipe with tremendous value when it comes to effort and taste. Start by getting your smoker to 225°F. Next, coat your chickens in olive oil and rub the dry herbs and seasoning salt all around it. Carefully place the chickens over the top of the open (half drank) beers and make sure they are stable. Let the chickens cook for about 2.5-3 hours or until the internal temperature reaches 165°F. Yup, it's that simple. Almost no work for something close to perfection.

There are handy beer can chicken contraptions now, or you can do it the old school way.

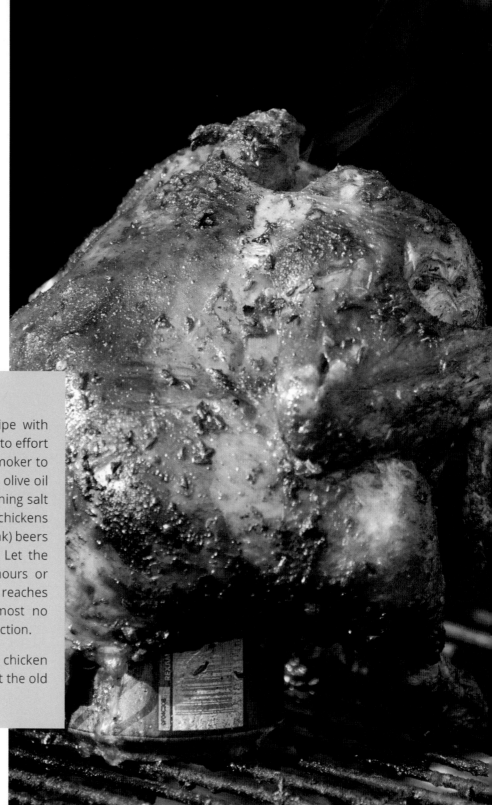

Kermit Cooked Up Miss Piggy

Ingredients:

- 2-3 Racks Country Style Ribs
- 2 Cups Barbecue Sauce
- Dry Rub
- 5 Tsps. Cumin
- ¼ Cup Salt
- ¼ Cup Pepper
- ⅓ Cup Sugar
- 2 Tbsp. Paprika
- 3 Tbsp. Chili Powder
- 2 Tbsp. Garlic Powder
- 2 Tbsp. Onion Powder
- 1 Cup Brown Sugar
- 1 Tsp. Red Pepper
- ½ Cup Honey

Instructions:

The most important step in this recipe has nothing to do with seasoning or pit temperature. It's removing the silver skin from the rib side of the ribs. Carefully do this with a paper towel and a sharp knife. This membrane doesn't break down during the cooking process which leads to a chewy experience, if you don't remove it now.

Start this recipe by mixing the dry rub in a large bowl. You'll want to have a shaker to store it in afterwards as this will be more than you probably need depending on how many racks you decide to cook. Apply the dry rub generously to the meat side of the ribs while saving a little for the rib side. Heat your grill to around 325°F and place the ribs on the grill, rib side down. Keep and eye on the pit as flare ups may occur. A little flame is good (it is your friend) but too much and you'll burn them in no time. Allow the ribs to cook over this heat for about 30 minutes. Reduce the heat to 250°F degrees and proceed to the next step.

For the next step, you'll want to have your foil read! Lay out an oversized sheet of foil for the size of the rack. Pour your honey out along the center line of the foil so that when you lay your ribs on them it will contact them from end to end. You'll also do this with 1 of the 2 cups of BBQ sauce. Once these two ingredients are on the foil, you'll bring the ribs over and put them meat side down on the foil. At this point the BBQ sauce and honey will be in contact with the meat side of the ribs. Wrap your foil tightly around the ribs (sometimes you'll need an additional sheet), and place the ribs back on the pit. You will cook them this way for another 45 minutes at 250°F. At the 45 minute mark, remove the ribs from the foil and place them back on the grill, rib side down. Using a brush, slather the remaining BBQ sauce over the meat. Cook for an additional 15-20 minutes then remove, cut and serve. This tangy, sweet, and savory meal will have them begging for more, so be sure to cook at least two racks!

Porkin' The Loin

Ingredients:

- 3-4 Lb. Pork Tenderloin (lean is fine because we'll be brining it)

Dry Rub:

- 5 Tsps. Cumin
- ¼ Cup Salt
- ¼ Cup Pepper
- ⅓ Cup Sugar
- 2 Tbsp. Paprika
- 3 Tbsp. Chili Powder
- 2 Tbsp. Garlic Powder
- 2 Tbsp. Onion Powder
- ⅓ Cup Brown Sugar
- 1 Tsp. Red Pepper

Brine Dry Rub:

- 6 Cups Water
- 2 Cups Apple Cider
- ¼ Cup Brown Sugar
- ⅓ Cup Kosher Salt
- 4 Tbsp. Black Peppercorns
- 1 Peeled Bulb Garlic
- 4 Tbsp. Rosemary
- 1 Tsp. Thyme
- Hawaiian Rolls
- Spicy Mustard

Instructions:

I'm a leftover fanatic! Don't get me wrong, I love to cook, but when I'm not cooking, then you know I'm eating. This dish is perfect hot or cold and tastes just as good on day 2 or 3... if it lasts that long!

Brining: The brining process adds moisture to the meat, so it can withstand the long smoking time and not get too dry to enjoy. Due to this, you'll need to do a little planning and have some patience. Wash your pork tenderloin and place it in a deep glass baking dish. Pour your brine mixture over the pork and make sure that the meat is completely submerged. I have a life and kids and a job, so if I brine something for 24 hours I feel damn near accomplished. If you can do 48 hours because your life is "organized", then absolutely go for it!

Now it's time to cook! Get your smoker to 250°F. Once the pit is ready, remove the tenderloin from the brine and pat it dry. Next, comes the dry rub. Cover the tenderloin completely in the dry rub and really pat it into the meat. Depending on the size of the meat, it can take anywhere from 3-8 hours to fully cook to an internal temperature of 145°F. Once it gets there, allow it to rest for at least 10 minutes before slicing. Personally, I prefer to slice thin and put it on a King's Hawaiian Roll with a little spicy mustard. If that's not your style, its wonderful on it's own with a side of beans, coleslaw, or even potato salad! Don't say I never taught you nothin'!

Don't Go Steakin' My Heart

Ingredients:

- 2 (2-inch) Beef Tenderloin Filets
- 2 Tbsp. Grapeseed Oil
- 2 Tbsp. Worcestershire Sauce
- 2 Tbsp. Cracked Black Pepper
- 1 Tbsp. Kosher Salt
- 1 Tbsp. Granulated Garlic
- 1 Tsp. Onion Powder

Instructions:

I use an infrared burner for this recipe as well as my grill. It's a little extra to do so but I love creating a crust on the meat, and with these being so thick, you'll want to also grill them at a lower temperature to get the internal temperature of the meat to 140°F

I also take a slightly different approach to seasoning these steaks. You'll want a couple of plates or dishes handy. First, add your Worcestershire sauce to the plate and roll your filets around in it. This will coat it completely and keep you from wasting or using too much Worcestershire sauce. It's a potent ingredient and too much will overpower the other flavors. Next, rub the meat with the grapeseed oil* and season it with the dry ingredients.

*Grapeseed oil is an important component to this dish and substituting it for olive oil or others can jeopardize the flavor profile negatively.

Make sure both your infrared burner and grill are on. You'll want your grill at 400°F and the infrared upwards of 600°F. Add your steaks and allow them to sear and begin to crust. The flame is your friend here, but keep an eye on them as the oil will promote some flare ups depending on your burner type. Turn them only once after a few minutes as that's all it should take to create a crust. Move them to the grill at this point and continue grilling them for 4-5 minutes on each side or until they reach an internal temperature of 140°F.

Allow the filets to rest for 5 minutes and serve. If you bought a prime cut, you'll be able to cut this with a fork. Enjoy that beautiful piece of meat.

You're A Real Fungi

:: Ingredients:

- 4 Portabella Mushrooms
- 4 Cloves Garlic
- 1 Tbsp. Thyme
- 1 Tbsp. Rosemary
- 1 Tsp. White Pepper
- 1 Tsp. Kosher Salt
- 1 Cup Italian Dressing

▼ Instructions:

If you're looking for a steak style dish but want to try something new, this is the recipe for you. Start this recipe by marinating your portabella mushrooms in italian dressing for a few hours. We're just adding a little flavor here so a few hours is plenty! Next, add your dry seasoning to both sides of the mushroom. Heat your grill to 400°F and toss these on. The italian dressing could cause some flare ups so keep an eye on things! Cook them on each side for about five minutes and remove them from the grill. They should be tender and easily cut with a fork or butterknife. While it's not filet mignon it is a great, and healthy option for those looking for something other than meat.

Made in the USA
Columbia, SC
06 December 2019